LIVING
on the
OTHER SIDE
of
GRIEF

DR. SETH W. CROSBY

A 40-Day Devotional & Workbook

ISBN: 978-1-965082-50-8

Publishing By:

The Acklin Group/ LERG EMPOWERMENT

www.lergempowermentusa.org

Editing/Design:

DemiCo National, LLC

www.DemiCoNational.com

Dedication & Introduction

I want to begin by thanking my wife and children for being there for me. Love you deeply.

To everyone who has ever walked through grief — and kept walking — this is for you.

I'm reminded of those last days of my mom's life in hospice. I would lay down on that pull-out couch at night, waking up every few hours just to see if she was still alive. Every morning, I whispered a prayer of thanks to God for one more day with her.

This devotional is for the brokenhearted.
For the ones who cry in silence.
For the ones who smile in public but mourn in private.
For those holding on by a thread, wondering if God still sees them.

I wrote this because I've been there. I know what it feels like to sit in the dark and wonder if the light will ever come back. I know how heavy life can feel when someone you love is no longer here. But I also know the faithfulness of God — even in the valley.

This isn't a quick fix. It's a companion for the journey. Each day of this devotional is meant to meet you right where you are — in the pain, in the questions, in the flickers of hope, and in the small steps it takes to breathe again.

You don't have to have it all figured out. You just have to keep showing up.

Let's walk this road together.

— Dr. Seth W. Crosby

Table of Contents

Day 1: When Grief First Hits

Scripture Focus: Psalm 34:18

KJV: "The Lord is nigh unto them that are of a broken heart; and saveth such as be of a contrite spirit."

NLT: "The Lord is close to the brokenhearted; He rescues those whose spirits are crushed."

AMPC: "The Lord is close to those who are of a broken heart and saves such as are crushed with sorrow for sin and are humbly and thoroughly penitent."

Devotional Teaching:

Grief doesn't send a warning before it arrives. It crashes into your life like a wave, flooding your soul with questions, sorrow, and silence. The moment grief first hits, it feels as if time freezes — like the world keeps moving, but you don't.

In that space, Scripture whispers one powerful truth: **God is near.**

He doesn't wait for you to be healed before He shows up — He draws close right in the middle of your heartbreak. He is near in the hospital room. He is near in the silence of your bedroom. He is near when the tears won't stop, and even when you feel numb.

Psalm 34:18 reminds us that *"The Lord is close to the brokenhearted and saves those who are crushed in spirit."* He leans in when the world pulls away. He is not distant or cold — He is personal and present. And even when you cannot feel Him, He is still faithful.

If grief is fresh in your life, take comfort in this: You don't have to have it all together to be held by God. You don't have to understand why it happened or where to go next. His nearness is not earned — it is promised.

Today, just breathe. You don't have to fix anything. You just have to let yourself be human... and **let God be God.**

Reflection Prompt:

What emotions have risen to the surface since grief first touched your life?

Can you remember moments when you clearly sensed God's nearness — or times when your heart longed for Him to be close?

Prayer Prompt:

God, I don't have the words right now. My heart is broken, and I don't know how to move forward. But You promise to be near the brokenhearted. Come close to me now. Be my comfort when I can't find answers. Help me breathe, and trust that You are here. Amen.

Day 2: God Sees Your Tears

Scripture Focus: Psalm 56:8

KJV: "Thou tellest my wanderings: put thou my tears into thy bottle: are they not in thy book?"

NLT: "You keep track of all my sorrows. You have collected all my tears in your bottle. You have recorded each one in your book."

AMPC: "You number and record my wanderings; put my tears into Your bottle—are they not in Your book?"

Devotional Teaching:

Tears are one of the rawest forms of human expression. They speak what words cannot. In grief, tears fall for many reasons — sorrow, confusion, anger, exhaustion, even gratitude. And sometimes, they come for no reason at all. That's okay. God doesn't just allow your tears — He treasures them.

Psalm 56:8 gives us a deeply personal glimpse into His heart: *"You have kept count of my tossings; put my tears in your bottle. Are they not in your book?"* God records your pain. He gathers your tears. He knows the nights your pillow has been soaked, and the moments you've swallowed tears just to make it through the day. Not one has gone unnoticed.

The world often tells us to "be strong" too soon, to move on before the heart is ready. But God says the opposite: *Bring your full sorrow to*

Me. You don't need to wipe your face or compose yourself before approaching Him. We don't have a distant God — we have a compassionate one who sees, remembers, and redeems even the smallest expression of our grief.

Your tears are not weakness. They are testimony. They declare that something mattered — that someone mattered. And even in this brokenness, your tears have a place in God's heart. You don't have to hold it all in. You are safe to let go — because every tear is held by the One who heals.

Reflection Prompt:

What kind of tears have you cried in this season — silent ones, angry ones, grateful ones, or something else?

How does it change your perspective to know that God collects and remembers every tear?

Prayer Prompt:

Lord, thank You for being the kind of God who sees me. Not just the parts of me that look okay, but the parts that are broken and grieving. Thank You for holding every tear I've cried. Help me trust that You are near, even in the moments I feel most alone. Amen.

Day 3: Honoring the Pain

Scripture Focus: Ecclesiastes 3:1, 4

KJV: "To everything there is a season, and a time to every purpose under the heaven: A time to weep, and a time to laugh; a time to mourn, and a time to dance."

NLT: "For everything there is a season, a time for every activity under heaven... A time to cry and a time to laugh. A time to grieve and a time to dance."

AMPC: "To everything there is a season, and a time for every matter or purpose under heaven... A time to weep and a time to laugh, a time to mourn and a time to dance."

Devotional Teaching:

We live in a world that rushes healing. There's pressure to *"move on,"* *"be strong,"* or *"get over it"* before the soul has even had time to breathe. But Scripture gives us permission to grieve — and even more than that, it shows us there is purpose in grief.

Ecclesiastes reminds us that there is a season for everything: joy and sorrow, weeping and dancing. That means mourning is not a mistake — it is a necessary part of healing. When we honor our pain instead of hiding from it, we open the door for God to meet us in it.

Grief is not something to conquer; it's something we carry with grace. The loss you've endured matters. The love that was shared matters. And the ache in your heart deserves space to be acknowledged.

To honor your pain is not weakness — it is to be human. Jesus wept. David mourned. Job sat in silence for days. Scripture never demands that you pretend. Instead, it invites you to be present, and to trust that this season is part of God's process.

You don't have to dance yet. You don't have to laugh today. But you are allowed to grieve — deeply, fully, and honestly — because grief is love's echo. And healing begins when we give ourselves permission to honor where we really are.

Reflection Prompt:

What would it look like to honor your grief today instead of suppressing it?

What pressures (from yourself or others) are making it hard to give your pain space?

Prayer Prompt:

God, help me to honor what I'm feeling without shame or guilt. Give me the strength to grieve without rushing, and the grace to know that You're with me in this season. I trust that in Your timing, the tears will turn — but today, I just need to be honest. And I believe that's okay. Amen.

Day 4: What to Do with the Silence

Scripture Focus: Psalm 46:10

KJV: "Be still, and know that I am God: I will be exalted among the heathen, I will be exalted in the earth."

NLT: "Be still, and know that I am God! I will be honored by every nation. I will be honored throughout the world."

AMPC: "Let be and be still, and know (recognize and understand) that I am God. I will be exalted among the nations! I will be exalted in the earth!"

Devotional Teaching:

There's a kind of silence that grief brings — the kind that sits heavy in a room, lingers in the pauses of conversation, and echoes deep in your soul. It can feel like everyone else has moved on while you're still frozen in a moment of time forgot. And in that silence, the question often rises: *Where is God?* But silence is not absence.

Psalm 46:10 doesn't call us to understand everything — it calls us to *be still.* Stillness is not the same as giving up; it's the surrender of trying to fix what we cannot control. It's the posture of a heart that says, *Even when I don't hear You, I trust that You are still here.*

Grief quiets the noise around us, and in that quiet, we come face-to-face with our emotions, our questions, and our God. It can feel uncomfortable, even painful. But silence can also become sacred. It is often the place where healing whispers begin.

You don't have to rush to fill every quiet moment. You don't have to force noise where God is asking for stillness. Sometimes the greatest comfort comes not through words, but in the simple assurance: He is still God. Still present. Still faithful. Still working. Even in the silence.

Reflection Prompt:

Have you experienced silence in your grief — from others or from God?

What would it mean for you to be still today, even without all the answers?

Prayer Prompt:

Lord, the silence has been hard. I've looked for You in the noise, but today I choose to find You in the stillness. Help me rest in the truth that You are near, even when You're quiet. I don't need all the answers — I just need to know You're here. Amen.

Day 5: You're Not Alone

Scripture Focus: Isaiah 41:10

KJV: "Fear thou not; for I am with thee: be not dismayed; for I am thy God: I will strengthen thee; yea, I will help thee; yea, I will uphold thee with the right hand of my righteousness."

NLT: "Don't be afraid, for I am with you. Don't be discouraged, for I am your God. I will strengthen you and help you. I will hold you up with my victorious right hand."

AMPC: "Fear not [there is nothing to fear], for I am with you; do not look around you in terror and be dismayed, for I am your God. I will strengthen and harden you to difficulties, yes, I will help you; yes, I will hold you up and retain you with My [victorious] right hand of rightness and Justice."

Devotional Teaching:

Grief can make you feel isolated — like you're carrying something too heavy for words. Even when people are near, the ache can be so deep that you feel invisible inside your pain. It's easy to wonder: *Does anyone really understand what I'm going through?* God does. And He says clearly: *"I am with you."*

Isaiah 41:10 is not just a call to be strong — it is a promise that you don't have to be strong alone. God offers His strength when yours runs out. He promises to hold you when you feel like slipping. He doesn't shy away from your brokenness; He steps into it with comfort, compassion, and unshakable presence.

You may feel overlooked by others, but you are never overlooked by God. He sees you. He hears your sighs. He knows the heaviness of your grief. Even when you cannot sense Him, His hand is holding you steady. You are not walking through this valley alone. The God who holds galaxies also holds your heart — and He is not going anywhere.

Reflection Prompt:

Have you felt alone in your grief journey?

What would it look like to lean into God's presence today, even if you don't "feel" Him?

Prayer Prompt:

Father, I've felt so alone in this pain. But Your Word reminds me that You

are here — not just watching, but holding me, helping me, and walking with me. Help me trust Your nearness, especially when I feel forgotten. Let me rest in the truth that I'm not alone. Amen.

Day 6: Blessed Are They That Mourn

Scripture Focus: Matthew 5:4

KJV: "Blessed are they that mourn: for they shall be comforted."

NLT: "God blesses those who mourn, for they will be comforted."

AMPC: "Blessed and enviably happy are those who mourn, for they shall be comforted!"

Devotional Teaching:

The world doesn't usually associate mourning with blessing. Mourning is messy, painful, and vulnerable. It's the moment you feel undone, shattered by loss, and unable to hide it. But in the kingdom of God, mourning isn't overlooked — it's honored.

Jesus said, "Blessed are they that mourn..." Why? Because God draws near to those who are broken. He doesn't just allow comfort — He promises it.

Grief may feel like a curse, but in God's hands, it becomes a path to deeper connection. When you mourn, you create space in your heart for God's comfort to take root. Not the kind of comfort that ignores your pain, but the kind that steps right into it and holds you there.

You may not feel "blessed" in your mourning. But God calls you blessed because of what He's doing in your heart — drawing you close, pouring out grace, and showing you His faithful presence when everything else feels uncertain.

This mourning will not last forever. But the comfort of God will carry you through it — one breath, one prayer, one promise at a time.

Reflection Prompt:

Have you ever felt God's comfort in your mourning?

If so, how did it show up?

What might it mean for your mourning to be "blessed"?

Prayer Prompt:

Jesus, You said I am blessed even when I mourn. Let me experience Your peace — not just around me, but deep within me. Amen.

Day 7: Where Do I Go From Here?

Scripture Focus: Proverbs 3:5–6

KJV: "Trust in the Lord with all thine heart; and lean not unto thine own understanding."

NLT: "Trust in the Lord with all your heart; do not depend on your own understanding."

AMPC: "Lean on, trust in, and be confident in the Lord with all your heart and He will direct and make straight and plain your paths."

Devotional Teaching:

One of the hardest questions after loss is: *Where do I go from here?*

Grief doesn't just touch your emotions — it shakes your direction. What once felt clear now feels uncertain. Dreams, routines, even your sense of self may feel blurred. You may not know what comes next — or if you're even ready to consider it, but the beautiful truth of Proverbs 3 is this: You don't have to figure out the whole path. You just have to trust the One who does.

God is not asking you to understand the *why* behind everything. He's asking you to trust His heart even when the map seems blank. When you're unsure how to move forward, He doesn't stand far off with a checklist — He comes close with compassion and wisdom.

The next step may be small. It may look like breathing, praying, or simply getting out of bed. But each step is a declaration of trust. And with every step, God promises to lead you — faithfully, gently, personally. You don't have to have all the answers today. Just stay close to the One who does. He will direct your path.

Reflection Prompt:

What parts of your future feel most uncertain right now?

What would it look like to trust God with the next step — not the whole path, just the next one?

Prayer Prompt:

God, I don't know where to go from here. Just show me the next step, and give me courage to take it. Amen.

Day 8: Small Steps, Still Progress

Scripture Focus: Psalm 56:13

KJV: "For thou hast delivered my soul from death: wilt not thou deliver my feet from falling"

NLT: "For you have rescued me from death; you have kept my feet from slipping."

AMPC: "For You have delivered my life from death, yes, and my feet from stumbling,"

Devotional Teaching:

When you're grieving, it can feel like everyone else is running while you can barely stand. You might look at your progress and feel like it's too small to matter — like healing should be faster, stronger, more complete by now. But God doesn't measure progress the way the world does.

Psalm 56:13 reminds us that even the act of walking — of putting one foot in front of the other — is part of what God sustains. If you got out of bed today, if you whispered a prayer, if you took one step forward despite the pain… that counts.

Small steps are still steps. And in seasons of sorrow, they matter more than ever. Each moment you choose to show up, to breathe, to believe that healing is possible — you're honoring both your pain and your progress.

Don't minimize what may feel slow. God sees the courage it takes to move through grief, not just past it. And He is walking with you — steadying your feet, guiding your path, and celebrating every brave step forward. You don't have to sprint. You don't even have to walk fast. Just keep moving — and trust that God is calling it progress.

Reflection Prompt:

What small steps have you taken that you haven't given yourself credit for?

Where do you need to give yourself permission to slow down in your healing?

Prayer Prompt:

God, sometimes I feel like I'm not moving fast enough through this pain. Help me stop comparing my pace to others — and trust that You're walking with me, one step at a time. Amen.

Day 9: Giving God the Broken Pieces

Scripture Focus: Psalm 34:18

KJV: "The Lord is nigh unto them that are of a broken heart; and saveth such as be of a contrite spirit."

NLT: "The Lord is close to the brokenhearted; He rescues those whose spirits are crushed."

AMPC: "The Lord is close to those who are of a broken heart and saves such as are crushed"

Devotional Teaching:

Grief has a way of shattering things — expectations, routines, even your sense of self. Some days, it feels like your heart is in pieces and your soul is too tired to try putting it all back together. But God isn't waiting for you to fix yourself. He's inviting you to bring Him the broken pieces.

Psalm 34:18 assures us that God comes close to the brokenhearted. Not just those who are healing — those who are still crushed. He doesn't require you to pull yourself together before He shows up. His comfort doesn't come after the cleanup — it starts in the middle of the mess.

There is no piece too jagged, no wound too raw, no question too loud for God to handle. He receives what's broken without judgment — and with the gentle care of a healer who restores what feels beyond repair.

You may not know how to heal, but you can start by handing God what hurts. The path to wholeness isn't built on pretending to be okay. It begins with honesty — and a God who's ready to take your sorrow, your questions, and your fragments… and start making something whole again.

Reflection Prompt:

What parts of your life or heart feel the most broken right now?

Are there any pieces you've been afraid to surrender to God?

Prayer Prompt:

Lord, I don't have much to give today — just broken pieces. I trust You with my pain. Amen.

Day 10: Peace Doesn't Mean Forgetting

Scripture Focus: Philippians 4:7

KJV: "And the peace of God, which passeth all understanding, shall keep your hearts and minds through Christ Jesus."

NLT: "Then you will experience God's peace, which exceeds anything we can understand."

AMPC: "And God's peace [shall be yours, that tranquil state of a soul assured of its salvation through Christ, shall garrison and mount guard over your hearts and minds in Christ Jesus."

Devotional Teaching:

For many who are grieving, peace can feel like betrayal. You finally catch your breath — and then the guilt creeps in.

"Am I forgetting them?"

"Does peace mean I've moved on?"

The answer is no. Peace is not forgetting. Peace is healing.

Philippians 4:7 speaks of a peace that "passes understanding" — not because it erases your pain, but because it coexists with it. This peace isn't logical. It doesn't always make sense, especially when your world has been shaken. But it is real.

Peace is God holding your heart steady when memories flood in. Peace is being able to laugh again without shame. Peace is knowing the loss was real — but so was the love — and nothing can take that from you.

You are not dishonoring your loved one by choosing to live. You are honoring them by carrying forward the love they gave. Peace isn't a sign that you've let go of them — it's a sign that God hasn't let go of you. You'll never forget. And you're not supposed to. But you can be whole again — and that doesn't erase the past. It simply means that grief doesn't have the final word. God's peace does.

Reflection Prompt:

Have you felt guilty for feeling peaceful or happy again at times?

How might embracing peace actually honor the memory of your loved one?

Prayer Prompt:

God, I've wrestled with peace. I trust that Your peace and my memories can live together. Amen.

Day 11: Taking Thoughts Captive

Scripture Focus: 2 Corinthians 10:5

KJV: "Casting down imaginations, and every high thing that exalteth itself against the knowledge of God, and bringing into captivity every thought to the obedience of Christ."

NLT: "We destroy every proud obstacle that keeps people from knowing God. We capture their rebellious thoughts and teach them to obey Christ."

AMPC: "[Inasmuch as we] refute arguments and theories and reasonings and every proud and lofty thing that sets itself up against the [true] knowledge of God; and we lead every thought and purpose away captive into the obedience of Christ (the Messiah, the Anointed One)."

Devotional Teaching:

Grief doesn't just affect your heart — it affects your mind. Thoughts race. Questions swirl. Lies try to settle in unnoticed: "It's my fault." "I should've done more." "Nothing will ever be okay again." If you're not careful, the thoughts that begin as passing fears can become permanent beliefs. That's why Scripture tells us to take every thought captive — not ignore them, but confront and surrender them. God knows your mind is a battlefield in this season. You're grieving a loss, and your thoughts are trying to make sense of something that may never fully make sense. That's exhausting. But He doesn't leave you defenseless.

Through Christ, you have the authority to challenge what isn't true. When a thought rises that contradicts God's heart — His love, His goodness, His promises — you can take hold of it and hand it to Him. You are not weak for struggling mentally during grief. You're human. And God has made provision for both your broken heart and your battling mind. Today, take one thought that's been haunting you — and hold it up to the light of God's truth. Does it reflect His love? His peace? His character? If not... it doesn't belong.

Reflection Prompt:

What thoughts have been the loudest in your mind since your loss?

Which ones do you need to surrender to the truth of Christ?

Prayer Prompt:

God, I've been overwhelmed by my thoughts — fears, regrets, and what-ifs. Help me recognize what's not from You. Give me the strength to take those thoughts captive and replace them with Your truth. I want my mind to be a place of peace, not torment. Amen.

Day 12: When You Feel Powerless

Scripture Focus: 2 Corinthians 12:9

KJV: "My grace is sufficient for thee: for my strength is made perfect in weakness."

NLT: "My grace is all you need. My power works best in weakness."

AMPC: "But He said to me, My grace (My favor and loving-kindness and mercy) is enough for you... for My strength and power are made perfect (fulfilled and completed) and show themselves most effective in [your] weakness."

Devotional Teaching:

Grief will make you feel powerless. You may have days where you can't think clearly. Where getting out of bed feels like a major victory. Where your prayers are more sighs than words. And in those moments, it's easy to believe the lie that weakness is failure. But God sees

weakness differently. In 2 Corinthians 12:9, God doesn't rebuke weakness — He meets it. He says, "My strength is made perfect in weakness." Not in performance. Not in perfection. In weakness. That means when you feel least capable, you're actually most eligible to receive God's strength. Not because you're trying harder — but because you've finally stopped trying to carry it alone.

Powerlessness in grief isn't something to be ashamed of. It's an opportunity to lean harder on the One who never runs out of strength. You don't have to fake it. You don't have to force it. You simply need to receive what only God can give. So if you feel like you can't keep going today — good news: God can. His strength is ready to carry you. Not when you feel strong again... but right now, in your weakness.

Reflection Prompt:

Where have you felt most powerless in this grief journey?

How does it change your perspective to know that God's strength is revealed in your weakness?

Prayer Prompt:

God, I'm tired of trying to be strong all the time. I feel powerless — but You say Your strength shows up right here. So I stop striving, and I ask You to carry me. Be strong in me today. I need You. Amen.

Day 13: Walking in Courage

Scripture Focus: Joshua 1:9

KJV: "Have not I commanded thee? Be strong and of a good courage... for the Lord thy God is with thee whithersoever thou goest."

NLT: "This is my command—be strong and courageous!... For the Lord your God is with you wherever you go."

AMPC: "Have I not commanded you? Be strong, vigorous, and very courageous... for the Lord your God is with you wherever you go."

Devotional Teaching:

Grief takes courage. Not just the kind of courage that shows up in big, loud moments — but the kind that whispers, "I'm still here," on days when it would be easier to quit. It takes courage to wake up. To face memories. To feel what hurts. To love again. To live again.

Joshua 1:9 wasn't spoken to someone who felt strong — it was spoken to someone who felt uncertain, maybe even afraid. Moses had died. Joshua was stepping into unfamiliar territory.

And God told him: You don't have to be fearless. You just have to walk forward — with Me. That's the same invitation God gives you today. You don't have to feel courageous to walk in courage. Courage isn't the absence of fear; it's moving anyway, knowing you're not alone. Your grief does not disqualify you from strength. In fact, your brokenness makes room for deeper dependence on the God who walks beside you. So if all you can do today is take one trembling step — that's courage. And heaven sees it.

Reflection Prompt:

What's one area in your grief journey where you've needed courage lately?

How can you remind yourself that God is walking with you?

Prayer Prompt:

Lord, I don't always feel brave, but I'm still moving. Help me walk in courage, even when fear whispers loud. Thank You for going with me — for holding my heart steady when everything around me feels uncertain. Strengthen me for today's steps. Amen.

Day 14: When the Memories Are Heavy

Scripture Focus: Lamentations 3:19–21

KJV: "I remember my affliction and my misery... This I recall to my mind, therefore have I hope."

NLT: "The thought of my suffering... Yet I still dare to hope when I remember this..."

AMPC: "I continually remember them and am bowed down... But this I recall and therefore have I hope..."

Devotional Teaching:

Grief has a memory. It shows up in places, in songs, in smells. It visits you during ordinary moments — folding laundry, walking past a photo, hearing a name. And sometimes, those memories bring warmth. But other times... they bring weight. You may find yourself smiling and crying in the same breath — unsure if remembering is helping or hurting. Jeremiah, the writer of Lamentations, knew this feeling. He remembered his pain so deeply it overwhelmed him. But in the same breath, he made a choice: "This I recall to my mind, therefore I have hope." What did he recall? The faithfulness of God. You don't have to stop remembering to move forward. Your memories are sacred. They're a part of your love story. But when they get heavy — when they threaten to sink you — you can also remember this: God is still good. He is still with you. He has not changed. There's room for both sorrow and hope in the same heart. You're not wrong for feeling the weight. But you're also not alone in carrying it. Let your memories live — but let your hope rise, too.

Reflection Prompt:

What memory has felt especially heavy lately?

What would it mean to hold that memory and God's hope at the same time?

Prayer Prompt:

God, You see the memories that flood my heart — some beautiful, some painful. Sometimes they lift me, and sometimes they bring me low. Help me carry them with grace. And when they feel too heavy, remind me of Your faithfulness. Let hope rise again. Amen.

Day 15: The Loneliness No One Sees

Scripture Focus: Psalm 27:10

KJV: "When my father and my mother forsake me, then the Lord will take me up."

NLT: "Even if my father and mother abandon me, the Lord will hold me close."

AMPC: "Although my father and my mother have forsaken me, yet the Lord will take me up [adopt me as His child]."

Devotional Teaching:

There's a kind of loneliness that grief brings that no one else can fully understand. You can be surrounded by people — kind people, helpful people — and still feel completely alone. Not because no one cares, but because no one can truly step into the space that person once filled. It's the quiet moments that ache the most. The empty seat. The missed phone call. The words you reach for and realize you no longer have someone to say them to. This is the loneliness no one sees. But God does. Psalm 27:10 reminds us that even when we feel abandoned — even when those we love are gone — the Lord holds us close. He doesn't just offer comfort from a distance. He gathers us in. He takes us up. He sits with us in the silence. God is not afraid of your loneliness. He doesn't rush you through it. Instead, He fills it with His presence. The comfort He offers is not always loud — but it is steady, faithful, and healing. You may feel invisible in your grief... but you are seen. You may feel forgotten... but you are held. God is with you — not just in the crowd, but especially in the quiet.

Reflection Prompt:

When have you felt the most unseen in your grief?

How does it feel to know that God draws close to you even there?

Prayer Prompt:

God, I've felt the ache of loneliness that words can't reach. Sometimes it feels like no one truly understands. But You see what others can't. You hold me when no one else knows I need it. Thank You for never leaving me alone in this pain. Amen.

Day 16: Anger in the Grief

Scripture Focus: Ephesians 4:26

KJV: "Be ye angry, and sin not: let not the sun go down upon your wrath."

NLT: "And don't sin by letting anger control you. Don't let the sun go down while you are still."

AMPC: "When angry, do not sin; do not ever let your wrath (your exasperation, your fury or indignation) last until the sun goes down."

Devotional Teaching:

No one warns you how angry grief can make you. Angry at what happened. Angry at who left. Angry at yourself. Even angry at God. This emotion can catch you off guard — especially if you've been taught that anger is wrong. But Scripture doesn't say don't be angry — it says, be angry, and sin not. In other words, anger is human — it's what you do with it that matters.

Anger often reveals pain that doesn't know where to go. It's your heart's way of saying, "This wasn't supposed to happen." It's valid. And God is not offended by your honesty. He invites it. God doesn't tell you to stuff your anger or pretend it's not there. He asks you to bring it to Him— fully, openly, and without shame. Because if anyone understands injustice, loss, and pain...it's Him. There's space at the cross for your sadness and

40

your fury. Your confusion and your cries. And as you release your anger — not onto others, but into God's hands — you begin to create room for healing. Anger is a part of grief. But it doesn't have to be the end of your story.

Reflection Prompt:

Have you experienced anger in your grief?

Who or what have you been angry at — even if you've never said it out loud?

Prayer Prompt:

God, I've held on to anger I haven't known what to do with. Some of it feels justified. Some of it feels confusing. But You already know it's there. I bring it to You — not to be punished, but to be healed. Help me process it with truth and grace. Amen.

Day 17: The "What Ifs" and "Why Nows"

Scripture Focus: Proverbs 3:5–6

KJV: "Trust in the Lord with all thine heart; and lean not unto thine own understanding. In all thy ways acknowledge him, and he shall direct thy paths."

NLT: "Trust in the Lord with all your heart; do not depend on your own understanding. Seek his will in all you do, and he will show you which path to take."

AMPC: "Lean on, trust in, and be confident in the Lord with all your heart and mind and do not rely on your own insight or understanding. In all your ways know, recognize, and acknowledge Him, and He will direct and make straight and plain your paths."

Devotional Teaching:

Grief is full of questions. What if I had done something differently? Why now? Why them? Why me?

These aren't just passing thoughts — they echo in your soul, keeping you up at night, chasing you in quiet moments. You may never say them out loud, but they live in the background of your healing. God never asks you to pretend those questions don't exist. But He does invite you not to lean on them. Proverbs 3:5–6 is not a command to ignore your pain —it's a lifeline when your understanding fails. It doesn't say, "You'll always know why." It says, "Trust in the Lord with all your heart." There will be things you never get answers to this side of eternity.

But your healing is not dependent on understanding — it's dependent on trusting the One who does. God can handle your "What ifs." He can sit with your "Why nows." He doesn't always remove the questions — but He promises to walk with you through them. You don't have to solve your way out of grief. You just have to lean — not on your own understanding, but on the arms of a God who sees the whole story.

Reflection Prompt:

What "what ifs" or "why nows" have followed you in your grief?

What would it look like to hand those questions to God without needing immediate answers?

Prayer Prompt:

God, I don't understand why things happened the way they did. I've asked questions that still echo with silence. But today, I'm choosing to lean — not on my own understanding, but on You. Hold me when I don't have answers. Be my peace in the mystery. Amen.

Day 18: A Different Kind of Healing

Scripture Focus: Psalm 147:3

KJV: "He healeth the broken in heart, and bindeth up their wounds."

NLT: "He heals the brokenhearted and bandages their wounds."

AMPC: "He heals the brokenhearted and binds up their wounds [curing their pains and their sorrows]."

Devotional Teaching:

When people talk about healing, they often picture a "return to normal" — a day when things feel like they used to, when the ache disappears, and everything falls back into place. But for those who've truly grieved, healing doesn't look like going back. It looks like learning how to live forward — with the loss, not in spite of it. God never promises that your heart will forget. He doesn't erase the past.

What He does promise is presence in the pain, and a process that restores what's been shattered. Psalm 147:3 says He heals the brokenhearted. That word "heal" doesn't mean "erase." It means to bind up, to tend to, to restore with care. Healing might mean you cry less often — but still cry. It might mean you laugh again — but carry a scar. It might mean you've learned how to hope again — even with a limp. This is a different kind of healing. It's not neat, but it's sacred. It's not fast, but it's real. God doesn't rush you. He doesn't demand perfection. He invites you to trust Him with each piece — and watch how His gentle hands do what time alone never could.

Reflection Prompt:

What did you expect healing to look like?

How is God showing you a different, more personal kind of healing?

Prayer Prompt:

God, I thought healing would look different. I thought it would feel like wholeness without any pain. But I see now that You're writing something deeper — a healing that still remembers, but also begins again. Help me trust Your process. Amen.

Day 19: When You Miss Them Most

Scripture Focus: John 11:35

KJV: "Jesus wept."

NLT: "Then Jesus wept."

AMPC: "Jesus wept."

Devotional Teaching:

Sometimes the ache of loss comes out of nowhere — and sometimes, it comes exactly when you expect it. A holiday. A birthday. An empty chair at the table. A smell, a song, a laugh that sounds just like theirs. Grief has no respect for timing. And even when you think you've "moved forward," it has a way of pulling you back into moments where all you can say is, "I miss them." And God understands that. Because Jesus wept too. In John 11, Jesus stood at the tomb of His friend Lazarus. Even though He knew resurrection was coming...He still cried. Why?

Because He felt the sorrow of those around Him. He felt the sting of death. He felt what we feel. That's the kind of Savior you have — one who weeps with you, not just one who rescues you. A Savior who doesn't silence your sadness, but sits in it with you. Missing someone deeply is not a sign that you're stuck. It's a sign that your love was real. And Jesus doesn't rush you through that — He weeps with you in it. Let the tears fall today if they need to. Jesus understands. And He's not going anywhere.

Reflection Prompt:

When do you feel their absence the most?

What do you wish you could say to them right now— and what do you need to hear from God in that place?

_____

Prayer Prompt:

Jesus, today I just miss them. The ache feels fresh all over again. Thank You for being a God who doesn't just watch me cry — but weeps with me. Remind me that I'm not alone, and let Your presence fill the empty spaces they once did. Amen.

Day 20: God, Are You Still Good?

Scripture Focus: Nahum 1:7

KJV: "The Lord is good, a strong hold in the day of trouble; and he knoweth them that trust in him."

NLT: "The Lord is good, a strong refuge when trouble comes. He is close to those who trust in him."

AMPC: "The Lord is good, a Strength and Stronghold in the day of trouble; He knows (recognizes, has knowledge of, and understands) those who take refuge and trust in Him."

Devotional Teaching:

Grief has a way of shaking everything — not just your emotions, but your faith. When the prayers you prayed weren't answered the way you hoped... When the loss came anyway...When the silence felt deafening... The question begins to rise in your heart: God, are You still good? You're not alone in that question. And asking it doesn't mean your faith is broken — it means you're human. Nahum 1:7 declares, "The Lord is good." Not only when life is good. Not only when prayers are answered. He is good in the day of trouble. He is a refuge, a shelter, a strength — even when you don't understand Him.

God's goodness is not dependent on your circumstances. It's part of His nature. And even when your world feels unrecognizable, He remains steady, trustworthy, and present. He doesn't shame you for your questions. He welcomes them. He doesn't punish your doubt. He draws closer. You don't need to deny your pain to declare His goodness. You can grieve and believe. You can weep and still whisper, "I trust You." The path back to peace starts with honesty — and leads to a God who's never stopped being good.

Reflection Prompt:

Have you questioned God's goodness during this season of grief?

What would it look like to trust His heart even when you don't understand His plan?

Prayer Prompt:

God, I've wrestled with this question: Are You still good? I don't always feel it. But I want to believe it again. Remind me of who You are — not just in my joy, but in my sorrow. Anchor my heart to Your goodness, even here. Amen.

Day 21: Letting Go of Guilt

Scripture Focus: Romans 8:1

KJV: "There is therefore now no condemnation to them which are in Christ Jesus, who walk not after the flesh, but after the Spirit."

NLT: "So now there is no condemnation for those who belong to Christ Jesus."

AMPC: "Therefore [there is] now no condemnation (no adjudging guilty of wrong) for those who are in Christ Jesus…"

Devotional Teaching:

Guilt is one of grief's most painful companions. It whispers: "You should've done more." "You shouldn't have said that." "If only you had gotten there sooner…" It replays moments in your mind and holds you hostage to what you can't go back and change. But the truth is this: God never asks you to carry what Jesus already covered. Romans 8:1 says there is no condemnation for those who are in Christ. None. Not even the quiet, hidden kind that comes wrapped in grief.

Yes — you may have regrets. Yes — things might have been left unsaid. But God is not shaming you. He's inviting you to grace. Guilt tries to keep you stuck in the past. But grace moves you forward — not by denying what happened, but by freeing you from the burden of trying to fix what you can't.

Letting go of guilt doesn't mean you don't care. It means you're surrendering the things you can't undo to the God who can redeem anything. You are allowed to be free. You are allowed to move forward. You are allowed to let go — not of the love, but of the guilt that was never yours to carry.

Reflection Prompt:

What regrets or "if only" thoughts have lingered in your grief?

What would it look like to release them into God's grace today?

Prayer Prompt:

God, You know the things I replay in my mind — the regrets, the moments I wish I could change. But Your Word says there's no condemnation for those who are in Christ. Help me believe that. Help me release the guilt I've been carrying. I choose to trust Your grace more than my memory. Amen.

Day 22: When Others Don't Understand

Scripture Focus: Romans 12:15

KJV: "Rejoice with them that do rejoice, and weep with them that weep."

NLT: "Be happy with those who are happy, and weep with those who weep."

AMPC: "Rejoice with those who rejoice [sharing others' joy], and weep with those who weep [sharing others' grief]."

Devotional Teaching:

One of the most isolating parts of grief is not just the loss itself — it's feeling like no one really understands. People say the wrong things. Or say nothing at all. They expect you to be "back to normal." They think your smile means you're "healed." Or they get uncomfortable when your tears still come. It's not always intentional — but it still hurts.

Romans 12:15 gives us a glimpse of what God desires from people: compassion that sits with you, not corrects you. God doesn't ask others to fix your grief — He asks them to weep with you in it.

But when others don't do that — when they don't understand or can't hold space — God still does. He never misreads your silence. He doesn't rush your process. And He won't walk away just because the world has moved on. Grief is a long road. Not everyone will journey the full length with you. And that's okay. Let your expectations shift — not your hope. Some people will surprise you with their love. Others will disappoint you with their distance. But God stays. Always.

Reflection Prompt:

Have you felt misunderstood in your grief — or judged for how you're grieving?

How can you give yourself permission to grieve honestly, even when others don't understand?

Prayer Prompt:

God, I've felt alone — not just because of the loss, but because of people who didn't know how to show up. Thank You for being a God who always understands, even when others don't. Help me forgive those who've hurt me in their silence, and surround me with those who reflect Your comfort. Amen.

Day 23: Grief in the Body

Scripture Focus: Matthew 11:28
KJV: "Come unto me, all ye that labour and are heavy laden, and I will give you rest."

NLT: "Then Jesus said, 'Come to me, all of you who are weary and carry heavy burdens, and I will give you rest.'"

AMPC: "Come to Me, all you who labor and are heavy-laden and overburdened, and I will cause you to rest. [I will ease and relieve and refresh your souls.]"

Devotional Teaching:
Grief doesn't just weigh on your heart — it lives in your body too.

It shows up in:
- Sleepless nights
- Headaches
- Tight shoulders
- Stomach aches
- A constant sense of fatigue

You may feel like you're falling apart for no reason — but there is a reason. Loss lives deep in your nervous system. You've been carrying invisible weight, and your body is trying to keep up.

Jesus speaks into this very place in Matthew 11:28. He doesn't just invite the spiritually tired — He calls to the weary, the burdened, the physically and emotionally exhausted. He says, *"Come to Me, and I will give you rest.*" Not just sleep — real rest. The kind that refreshes your soul, calms your body, and speaks peace into your very bones.

You don't have to ignore what your body is telling you. You're not weak for needing rest. You are human. And God knows how to tend not just to your spirit, but to your body as well.

So exhale. Let your shoulders drop. Drink some water. Take a walk. Cry if you need to. And let your body know: **God is here, and He is restoring me — one breath at a time.**

Reflection Prompt:
How has grief shown up in your body — fatigue, tension, sleep, appetite, or health?

What does your body need right now that you may have been ignoring?

Prayer Prompt:
Jesus, I've been carrying more than I realized. My body feels the weight, even when I try to keep going. Help me slow down. Help me care for this vessel You gave me. Let Your rest settle into the places that ache. Amen.

Day 24: What Grief Has Taught Me

Scripture Focus: —Psalm 119:71

KJV: "It is good for me that I have been afflicted; that I might learn thy statutes."

NLT: "My suffering was good for me, for it taught me to pay attention to your decrees."

AMPC: "It is good for me that I have been afflicted, that I might learn Your statutes."

Devotional Teaching:

Grief changes you.

Not just on the outside, but deep in the hidden places of your soul. At first, it may feel like all it's done is take — your joy, your confidence, your rhythm, your sense of self. But in time… something else emerges: wisdom, perspective, strength, compassion, and clarity.

Psalm 119:71 doesn't deny the pain of affliction — it simply recognizes that even pain has something to teach us. That doesn't mean the loss was good. It means God can bring good even from what broke you.

Grief teaches you what matters most. It teaches you how to slow down. It teaches you how to hold space for others. It teaches you to depend on God in ways that comfort never could. The lesson isn't that you had to go through it to grow — it's that since you went through it, God isn't going to waste a single drop of it.

Let today be a moment of quiet reflection. What has grief taught you? Not because you asked for it — but because even here, you are being shaped into someone deeper, more anchored, more whole.

Reflection Prompt:
What have you learned about yourself, God, or life during this grief journey?

How might your pain shape your purpose moving forward?

Prayer Prompt:
God, I wouldn't have chosen this path — but since I'm here, teach me through it. Open my eyes to the ways You're growing me in the middle of the pain. Thank You for being the kind of God who brings purpose out of sorrow. Amen.

Day 25: Worship in the Weeping

Scripture Focus: Job 1:21

KJV: "The Lord gave, and the Lord hath taken away; blessed be the name of the Lord."

NLT: "The Lord gave me what I had, and the Lord has taken it away. Praise the name of the Lord!"

AMPC: "The Lord gave and the Lord has taken away; blessed, praised, and magnified in worship be the name of the Lord!"

Devotional Teaching:

Worship doesn't always sound like singing. Sometimes it sounds like silence — or sobs — or whispered prayers through tears. Sometimes it looks like lifting empty hands and saying, "God, I still trust You... even here."

Job's words in Job 1:21 were not spoken in joy. They were spoken from deep loss. He had just lost nearly everything — his children, his wealth, his security. And still, he said, "Blessed be the name of the Lord." That is worship in its rawest form.

Grief does not cancel your ability to worship. In fact, it may be the most sacred offering you ever give. Not because you're ignoring the pain — but because you're choosing to trust God with it.

Worship in the weeping is not about feeling strong. It's about remembering who God is when everything else feels uncertain. It's about declaring that He's still worthy — not because of what He gives, but because of who He is.

So today, you don't have to sing loud. You don't have to pretend to be okay. You can bring your grief into His presence and still choose to say: "God, You are good. You are with me. And I will praise You — even in this."

Reflection Prompt:
What does worship look like for you in this season of grief?

Is it hard to praise God while you're still in pain?

Prayer Prompt:
God, sometimes all I have to offer is my tears. But I bring them to You as worship. Not because I understand everything — but because I still believe You're worthy. Let my weeping be worship. Let my brokenness be a song. I trust You, even here. Amen.

Day 26: When It's Hard to Pray

Scripture Focus: Romans 8:26

KJV: "Likewise the Spirit also helpeth our infirmities: for we know not what we should pray for as we ought: but the Spirit itself maketh intercession for us with groanings which cannot be uttered."

NLT: "And the Holy Spirit helps us in our weakness. For example, we don't know what God wants us to pray for. But the Holy Spirit prays for us with groanings that cannot be expressed in words."

AMPC: "So too the [Holy] Spirit comes to our aid and bears us up in our weakness; for we do not know what prayer to offer... but the Spirit Himself goes to meet our supplication and pleads in our behalf with unspeakable yearnings and groanings too deep for utterance."

Devotional Teaching:

There are days when prayer feels natural — when the words flow easily and faith feels strong, but then there are days when the grief is too thick... and the words are just gone.

All you have is a sigh, a whisper, a tear, a silence that aches.

You may wonder, Is that enough? According to Romans 8:26 — yes. When you can't find the words, the Holy Spirit intercedes for you. He carries your groans to the Father. He translates your silence into a sacred plea. He speaks the words your heart is too weary to form. God doesn't demand perfect prayers — He desires honest presence. So, if all you can do today is sit with Him in silence... you've prayed. If all you can offer is a deep breath or a tear... that's enough. Prayer isn't a performance — it's a connection. And even when your words fail, your soul still speaks. And your Father still listens.

Reflection Prompt:

Have you experienced seasons where it was hard to pray?

What might God be saying to you in the silence?

Prayer Prompt:

God, I don't have the words right now. My heart is tired. My mind is scattered. But I believe You're still near — even in the silence. Let Your Spirit pray for me when I don't know how. And let that be enough. Amen.

Day 27: Forgiving in the Wake of Loss

Scripture Focus: Ephesians 4:32

KJV: "And be ye kind one to another, tenderhearted, forgiving one another, even as God for Christ's sake hath forgiven you."

NLT: "Instead, be kind to each other, tenderhearted, forgiving one another, just as God through Christ has forgiven you."

AMPC: "And become useful and helpful and kind to one another, tenderhearted (compassionate, understanding, loving-hearted), forgiving one another [readily and freely], as God in Christ forgave you."

Devotional Teaching:

Grief can uncover wounds you didn't expect to face — especially when people disappoint you in your pain. Maybe someone wasn't there when you needed them. Maybe words were spoken at the worst possible time. Maybe unresolved issues with the person you lost are now impossible to fix. And now you're left with grief in one hand... and anger or hurt in the other. Forgiveness in the wake of loss doesn't mean you pretend nothing happened. It means you choose to release the weight of offense so it doesn't poison your healing.

Ephesians 4:32 doesn't call us to forgive because it's easy. It calls us to forgive because we've been forgiven — fully, freely, and tenderly. And the same grace that saved you can also strengthen you to extend grace, even when it's hard.   Forgiveness doesn't excuse the hurt.

It doesn't mean reconciliation is always possible. But it does mean you're letting go of what's keeping you bound. Forgiveness may not come all at once. It may take time. But each step you take to release the pain is also a step toward your own peace.

Reflection Prompt:

Is there anyone you've struggled to forgive during your grief — a friend, family member, even the one you lost?

What's one small step you can take toward releasing that burden?

Prayer Prompt:

Father, You know the hurt I've carried. Some wounds were made deeper by what others said or didn't say. I don't want to stay stuck in anger. Teach me how to forgive — not because it's easy, but because I want to be free. Give me grace to release what I can't change. Amen.

Day 28: Becoming Someone New

Scripture Focus: 2 Corinthians 5:17

KJV: "Therefore if any man be in Christ, he is a new creature: old things are passed away; behold, all things are become new."

NLT: "This means that anyone who belongs to Christ has become a new person. The old life is gone; a new life has begun!"

AMPC: "Therefore if any person is [engrafted] in Christ...the old [previous moral and spiritual condition] has passed away. Behold, the fresh and new has come!"

Devotional Teaching:

Grief doesn't just change your circumstances — it changes you. There comes a moment, somewhere deep in the journey, when you look in the mirror and realize: I'm not the same person I was before the loss. And that realization can feel disorienting. You may miss the version of yourself that laughed more easily, trusted more quickly, or felt more confident. But what if the new you — the one shaped by pain, softened by empathy, and anchored by God — is just as beautiful?

2 Corinthians 5:17 reminds us that transformation is part of God's promise. He doesn't just patch up the old you — He births something new. Grief can become holy ground for this rebirth. Not because you wanted the pain, but because even in pain, God is doing something eternal. You're not going back to "who you were." And that's okay. You are becoming

someone deeper. Wiser. Stronger. You're becoming someone who has walked through loss... and still believes in life.

Reflection Prompt:

How has grief changed you?

In what ways are you becoming someone new — spiritually, emotionally, or relationally?

Prayer Prompt:

God, I don't always recognize who I am anymore — but I trust You're still at work in me. Thank You for staying close while I grieve, and for shaping something new from what I've lost. Help me embrace who I'm becoming with grace and courage. Amen.

Day 29: Seeing Beauty Again

Scripture Focus: —Isaiah 61:3

KJV: "To appoint unto them that mourn in Zion, to give unto them beauty for ashes, the oil of joy for mourning, the garment of praise for the spirit of heaviness..."

NLT: "To all who mourn in Israel, he will give a crown of beauty for ashes, a joyous blessing instead of mourning, festive praise instead of despair..."

AMPC: "To grant [consolation and joy] to those who mourn in Zion— to give them an ornament (a garland or diadem) of beauty instead of ashes, the oil of joy instead of mourning, the garment [expressive] of praise instead of a heavy, burdened, and failing spirit..."

Devotional Teaching:

There comes a time in your grief when beauty begins to whisper again. Not loud or sudden. Not in a way that demands your healing. But in quiet ways — a sunrise, a laugh you didn't expect, a moment of peace you didn't plan. At first, you might feel guilty for enjoying it. Am I allowed to smile again? What if they think I've moved on too quickly? Does this mean I'm forgetting? But Isaiah 61:3 tells us that beauty for ashes is a gift from God — not a betrayal of our grief. It's His promise to those who mourn: You won't live in ashes forever.

Beauty doesn't erase the pain. It grows beside it.It reminds you that even here — especially here — God is still present, still kind, still offering you glimpses of redemption. Seeing beauty again doesn't mean the sorrow is gone. It means your soul is learning how to carry both — joy and grief, pain and praise — in the same hands.

Reflection Prompt:

Where have you seen unexpected beauty in this season?

How did it feel?

Did it bring joy, guilt, comfort — or all three?

Prayer Prompt:

Father, thank You for every glimpse of beauty You've given me, even in my sorrow. Help me receive them as gifts, not as guilt. Let me see Your goodness in the little things again. Heal my heart so I can hold both pain and praise with grace. Amen.

Day 30: I'm Still Here for a Reason

Scripture Focus: Jeremiah 29:11

KJV: "For I know the thoughts that I think toward you, saith the Lord, thoughts of peace, and not of evil, to give you an expected end."

NLT: "'For I know the plans I have for you,' says the Lord. 'They are plans for good and not for disaster, to give you a future and a hope.'"

AMPC: "For I know the thoughts and plans that I have for you, says the Lord, thoughts and plans for welfare and peace and not for evil, to give you hope in your final outcome."

Devotional Teaching:

There are moments in grief when you wonder why you're still here. Why you're the one still breathing. Why God didn't stop the loss. He didn't take you instead. Those questions are deeply human. They come from a place of pain — a longing to understand what feels senseless.

But here's what's true:

If you're still here, it's because you're still called. Your breath is proof that God isn't finished writing your story. Yes, the loss changed you. Yes, the pain is real.

But your life still carries purpose — not just in spite of grief, but because of it. There are people who need the compassion your pain taught you. There are prayers you're still meant to pray. There are dreams that still carry your name. Jeremiah 29:11 wasn't written for people in comfort — it was spoken to exiles, people who had lost so much. And still, God said: I have plans for you... to give you a future and a hope. If you're still here... it's on purpose. There's more life to live. And God will walk with you into it.

Reflection Prompt:

Have you ever struggled to believe your life still has purpose after loss?

What gives you hope that God is not done with your story?

Prayer Prompt:

God, some days I wonder why I'm still here. But I choose to believe You still have purpose for me. Remind me that my life matters. Show me how to live fully — not just survive. Give me hope for the future You've written just for me. Amen.

Day 31: Breathing Again

Scripture Focus: Job 33:4

KJV: "The Spirit of God hath made me, and the breath of the Almighty hath given me life."

NLT: "For the Spirit of God has made me, and the breath of the Almighty gives me life."

AMPC: "[It is] the Spirit of God that made me [which has stirred me up], and the breath of the Almighty that gives me life [which inspires me]."

Devotional Teaching:

There's something sacred about the first time you notice yourself breathing again — not just surviving, but living.Grief has a way of tightening your chest.Of holding your breath without meaning to.Of moving through the day in a fog where even inhaling feels like effort.But then — sometimes quietly, sometimes suddenly — you notice the air filling your lungs again. Not with all the answers. Not without pain. But with something that feels like... life.Job 33:4 reminds us: It is the breath of God that gives life.Not just at birth, but again... and again... and again.His breath revives you in the deepest valleys. His Spirit whispers into the places you thought were too weary to live again.Today isn't about fixing everything. It's about noticing that you're still here — still breathing — and letting that be enough for now.You don't have to rush ahead. You don't have to "move on." You just have to breathe… and let grace meet you in this moment.

Reflection Prompt:

Have you noticed any recent moments where life felt a little lighter — where it felt like you were breathing again?

Prayer Prompt:

God, thank You for the breath in my lungs today. Some days it's hard to keep going, but I trust that each breath is a reminder that You're still with me. Breathe fresh life into me — physically, emotionally, spiritually — and give me the strength to live again. Amen.

Day 32: When the Tears Won't Stop

*Scripture Focus:*Psalm 56:8

KJV:"Thou tellest my wanderings: put thou my tears into thy bottle: are they not in thy book?"

NLT:"You keep track of all my sorrows. You have collected all my tears in your bottle. You have recorded each one in your book."

AMPC:"You number and record my wanderings; put my tears into Your bottle—are they not in Your book?"

Devotional Teaching:

There are days when tears come without warning — in the middle of a sentence, a song, a silence.Tears you thought you were done crying.Tears that speak what your mouth cannot.And maybe you've wondered: Does anyone really see?Does God notice this pain I can't even explain?Psalm 56:8 gives us a beautiful, tender answer:God keeps every tear.He doesn't rush you to dry them. He collects them — treasures them.Not one of them is wasted. Not one goes unnoticed.Each tear is a sentence in your story, and He has recorded every single one.You don't have to be ashamed of your tears. They are sacred.They are proof that you have loved deeply.And healing isn't the absence of tears — it's knowing that even in your weeping, you are not alone.So if today is one of those tear-soaked days... let them fall.And let the God who catches them also comfort you.

Reflection Prompt:

What do your tears say that words can't?

Do you believe God sees and values even your silent pain?

_____

Prayer Prompt:

Lord, You see every tear I cry — even the ones I try to hide. Thank You for never making me feel ashamed of them. I give You my pain, my grief, and the tears that won't stop. Catch them, hold me, and carry me through. Amen.

Day 33: Permission to Live After Loss

*Scripture Focus:*Psalm 118:17

KJV:"I shall not die, but live, and declare the works of the Lord."

NLT:"I will not die; instead, I will live to tell what the Lord has done."

AMPC:"I shall not die but live, and shall declare the works and recount the illustrious acts of the Lord."

Devotional Teaching:

Grief can leave you feeling like part of you died with the one you lost.And while their life was precious and unforgettable, you may silently wonder… "Is it wrong for me to live fully again?"There can be a strange kind of guilt in surviving.In laughing again.In planning again.In dreaming again.But today's scripture is a bold declaration: "I shall not die, but live."And not just survive, but live to declare the goodness of God.Living doesn't mean forgetting.Joy doesn't mean betrayal.Healing doesn't mean you've erased the love.You're not dishonoring their memory by living.In fact, living well because of what you've learned through grief might be one of the greatest ways to honor them.God is not asking you to rush your healing.But He is inviting you to give yourself permission — to believe that your story is not over.There is still life ahead of you.And you have a right to receive it.

Reflection Prompt:

Have you ever felt guilty for laughing, dreaming, or enjoying life again?

What would it look like to give yourself permission to live?

_____

Prayer Prompt:

God, sometimes it's hard to embrace life again. I don't want to forget, and I don't want to feel like I'm leaving my loved one behind. But I also know You still have purpose for me. Help me accept joy again. Help me live again. Amen.

Day 34: Learning to Rest Again

*Scripture Focus:*Matthew 11:28

KJV:"Come unto me, all ye that labour and are heavy laden, and I will give you rest."

NLT:"Then Jesus said, 'Come to me, all of you who are weary and carry heavy burdens, and I will give you rest.'"

AMPC:"Come to Me, all you who labor and are heavy-laden and overburdened, and I will cause you to rest. [I will ease and relieve and refresh your souls.]"

Devotional Teaching:

Grief is exhausting — not just emotionally, but physically, spiritually, and mentally.It wears on the soul like a weight you never asked to carry.And even after the funeral ends… the weight often doesn't.So you keep pushing. You keep doing. You keep showing up — even while breaking on the inside.But God's invitation isn't to "do more."It's not "push through."It's not "be strong."It's simple: "Come to Me, and I will give you rest."Not escape.Not denial.But true rest — soul-deep, life-renewing rest that only He can give.Rest doesn't mean you're weak.It means you're human.And it means you trust God enough to lay down your burdens and let Him carry them — even for a moment.Today, you don't have to have it all together.You're allowed to rest.You're allowed to breathe.Grief may be part of your journey, but it doesn't have to consume all of your strength.Let God refresh you.

Reflection Prompt:

How has grief impacted your ability to rest — physically, mentally, or spiritually?

What does real rest look like for you right now?

Prayer Prompt:

Jesus, I come to You weary and burdened. I'm tired in ways I can't always explain. Help me lay it all down and receive Your rest — the kind that renews my soul and gives me strength for tomorrow. Amen.

Day 35: The Quiet Strength Within

*Scripture Focus:*Isaiah 40:31

KJV:"But they that wait upon the Lord shall renew their strength; they shall mount up with wings as eagles; they shall run, and not be weary; and they shall walk, and not faint."

NLT:"But those who trust in the Lord will find new strength. They will soar high on wings like eagles. They will run and not grow weary. They will walk and not faint."

AMPC:"But those who wait for the Lord [who expect, look for, and hope in Him] shall change and renew their strength and power…"

Devotional Teaching:

Grief has a way of making us feel weak — like every step forward takes more energy than we have.But there is a strength that doesn't shout.A strength that doesn't need applause.A strength that doesn't look like "having it all together" — but looks like showing up when it hurts.This is quiet strength.And it comes from waiting on the Lord.Waiting doesn't mean passively sitting back — it means trusting, even when you can't see the outcome.It means leaning in, holding on, and letting His strength rise within you.You may not feel strong.But look at all you've made it through.Look at how you've continued to breathe, to rise, to love, to pray — even with a broken heart.That's not a weakness.That's

God's strength alive in you.It may be quiet...But it's powerful.And it's more than enough to carry you forward.

Reflection Prompt:

What are some quiet ways God has given you strength in this season?

How do you see yourself continuing to grow stronger, even in the waiting?

Prayer Prompt:

Lord, I thank You for the quiet strength You give — the kind that doesn't always show on the outside but keeps me steady on the inside. Help me keep trusting, keep waiting, and keep walking with You. Amen.

Day 36: Rebuilding What Was Lost

Scripture Focus: Joel 2:25a

KJV: "And I will restore to you the years that the locust hath eaten…"

NLT: "The Lord says, 'I will give you back what you lost to the swarming locusts…'"

AMPC: "And I will restore or replace for you the years that the locust has eaten…"

Devotional Teaching:

Grief doesn't just break hearts — it can break routines, relationships, finances, dreams, and a sense of identity. Sometimes, it feels like life will never be whole again. But we serve a God of restoration. He doesn't ignore what was lost — He promises to restore it. Not always in the same way. Not always on our timeline. But always with purpose. God sees the gaps. The empty places. The plans that didn't get fulfilled. And He's not asking you to put it all back together by yourself. He's saying: "Let Me help you rebuild."

Maybe it won't look exactly like before. Maybe it will be something new, something deeper, something more rooted in grace. But you won't stay in ruins. This is not the end of your story. It's the beginning of a new chapter — one God is helping you build, piece by piece.

Reflection Prompt:

What areas of your life feel like they've been "eaten away" by grief?

Where do you sense God might be beginning to rebuild?

_____

Prayer Prompt:

Father, there are places in my life that feel broken beyond repair. But I trust You to restore what I cannot. Thank You for being the God who rebuilds, redeems, and makes things new. Help me believe again. Amen.

Day 37: Permission to Feel Joy

Scripture Focus: Psalm 16:11

KJV: "Thou wilt shew me the path of life: in thy presence is fullness of joy…"

NLT: "You will show me the way of life, granting me the joy of your presence and the pleasures of living with you forever."

AMPC: "You will show me the path of life; in Your presence is fullness of joy, at Your right hand there are pleasures forevermore."

Devotional Teaching:

Grief and joy can feel like opposites. When loss enters your life, joy may feel out of reach — or even inappropriate.

You may have asked yourself:

"Is it wrong to laugh again?"

"Will people think I've moved on too fast?"

"Does feeling joy mean I've forgotten who I lost?"

The answer is no. Joy does not erase grief. It simply reminds your soul that pain is not the only voice that gets to speak. Joy is not betrayal.

It's survival. It's proof that your heart is still alive. It's a gift from God —
a whisper of heaven in the middle of sorrow. You are not dishonoring your
loved one by smiling again. You are honoring what they meant to you by
choosing to live. So today, give yourself permission to laugh. To sing. To
dance. To feel joy — even if it's momentary. This is not forgetting. This is
healing.

Reflection Prompt:

Do you struggle with guilt around feeling joy after your loss?

What would it look like to allow space for joy in your healing journey?

Prayer Prompt:

God, I've been afraid to feel joy again. But I know joy is not denial — it's
part of the healing. Help me make room for moments of joy without guilt.
Fill me with Your presence and Your peace. Amen.

Day 38: Holding the Memory, Living the Moment

Scripture Focus: Ecclesiastes 3:1

KJV: "To every thing there is a season, and a time to every purpose under the heaven..."

NLT: "For everything there is a season, a time for every activity under heaven."

AMPC: "To everything there is a season, and a time for every matter or purpose under heaven..."

Devotional Teaching:

There's a sacred tension between remembering the past and living in the present. Sometimes, it feels like you have to choose — either hold tightly to the memory or let go so you can move on. But grief isn't that black-and-white. You can honor the memory and embrace the moment. You can love what was and still live in what is. God doesn't ask you to forget. He invites you to carry the memory with grace — not as a weight, but as a witness to what you've been through and what He's brought you through.

That memory doesn't have to keep you stuck. It can become fuel for compassion, for hope, for healing — and yes, for living. The moment you're in now is sacred too. It deserves your attention. Your breath. Your presence. So today, take the memory with you — but also open your hands to what this moment has to offer. You are still here. And that means life is still happening — one day, one breath, one purpose at a time.

Reflection Prompt:

What is one memory you want to carry forward — not as a burden, but as a beautiful part of your story?

How can you honor that memory while being present today?

Prayer Prompt:

Lord, help me balance memory and presence. Teach me how to carry the love without clinging to the pain. Help me live fully in this moment, even as I hold what matters from the past. Amen.

Day 39: It Doesn't Have to Be Perfect to Be Beautiful

Scripture Focus: 2 Corinthians 12:9a

KJV: "My grace is sufficient for thee: for my strength is made perfect in weakness..."

NLT: "My grace is all you need. My power works best in weakness..."

AMPC: "My grace (My favor and loving-kindness and mercy) is enough for you... for My strength and power are made perfect (fulfilled and completed) and show themselves most effective in [your] weakness."

Devotional Teaching:

In grief, you may find yourself chasing after "okay." Trying to make things feel normal. Trying to look like you're healing the "right way." But healing is not linear. It's not always neat. And it's definitely not perfect.

There are days you'll feel strong — and days when even breathing feels like a battle. There will be smiles that feel real and some that you have to push through. There will be tears, setbacks, messiness, and moments you don't have the words to explain. And still — God is there. Still — healing is happening. God doesn't need your journey to be polished.

He wants it to be honest. Because that's where His grace shows up: In the broken places. In the quiet ache. In the unedited story. So if today doesn't feel like a victory, it's okay. If your process isn't tidy, that's alright. You're not behind. You're not failing. You're healing — and that is beautiful. Even if it's imperfect.

Reflection Prompt:

Have you felt pressure to "grieve well" or to appear stronger than you are?

How can you begin to embrace the beauty in your real, unpolished healing process?

Prayer Prompt:

God, thank You that I don't have to pretend to be okay for You to love me. Remind me that even in weakness, Your grace is working. Help me to rest in the truth that I'm healing — even when it's messy. Amen.

Day 40 This Is Not the End of My Story

Scripture Focus: Philippians 1:6

KJV: "Being confident of this very thing, that he which hath begun a good work in you will perform it until the day of Jesus Christ."

NLT: "And I am certain that God, who began the good work within you, will continue his work until it is finally finished…"

AMPC: "And I am convinced and sure of this very thing, that He Who began a good work in you will continue until the day of Jesus Christ [developing, perfecting, and bringing it to full completion in you]."

Devotional Teaching:

Grief may have changed your story — but it hasn't ended it. Loss has a way of putting life on pause. It feels like everything stops while the world keeps spinning. You may have wondered if the best parts of your life were behind you. If your purpose died with your loss. If joy, meaning, or peace could ever come back.

But hear this truth:

God is not finished with you. If you're still breathing, He's still building. Your story is still unfolding — and even the painful chapters are not wasted. They are part of your testimony. They are shaping your character. They are softening your heart. They are pointing to a God who restores, redeems, and resurrects. This is not where your story ends. It's where a new chapter begins. So walk forward — not forgetting the past, but trusting that your future still holds purpose, beauty, and promise. Let your life speak: "This is not the end."

Reflection Prompt:

How has grief tried to convince you that your story is over?

What is one area where you're beginning to hope again?

Prayer Prompt:

God, thank You for reminding me that You're not done with me. Even in the hardest moments, You've stayed near. I choose to trust that my story is still unfolding, and You are writing something beautiful with my life. Amen.

Ending Encouragement

You've made it to Day 40 — and that is no small thing. But I want to remind you: this isn't the end of your story. Grief may have changed your life, but it doesn't define your future. There is still purpose in you. There is still hope ahead. There is still a reason you're here — and it's not by accident. Healing doesn't mean forgetting. Joy doesn't mean betrayal. And moving forward doesn't mean you're leaving anyone behind. It means you're trusting God with the next chapter. So take your time. Feel what you need to feel. But don't stop living. You are still here for a reason.

And your life still speaks. Let your story say: "This is not the end."

About the Author

Dr. Seth W. Crosby is a teacher, author, and mentor called to encourage people through faith, healing, and purpose. As the voice behind the movement "It's My Time," Dr. Crosby inspires others to rise from life's hard places with truth, courage, and grace. His heart beats for those who feel forgotten or broken, and his message is simple: God is not finished with you yet.

www.ingramcontent.com/pod-product-compliance
Lightning Source LLC
Chambersburg PA
CBHW061708120626
46550CB00003B/1145